North American Indians Today

North American Indians Today

Apache

Cherokee

Cheyenne

Comanche

Creek

Crow

Huron

Iroquois

Navajo

Ojibwa

Osage

Potawatomi

Pueblo

Seminole

Sioux

North American
Indians Today

Navajo

by
Kenneth McIntosh

Mason Crest Publishers

Philadelphia

Mason Crest Publishers Inc.
370 Reed Road
Broomall, Pennsylvania 19008
(866) MCP-BOOK (toll free)

First printing
1 2 3 4 5 6 7 8 9 10
Library of Congress Cataloging-in-Publication Data on file at the Library of Congress.
ISBN: 1-59084-672-9
1-59084-663-X (series)

Design by Lori Holland.
Composition by Bytheway Publishing Services, Binghamton, New York.
Cover design by Benjamin Stewart.
Printed and bound in the Hashemite Kingdom of Jordan.

Photography by Benjamin Stewart. Pictures on pp. 6, 74 courtesy of Keith Rosco; pp. 15, 18, 20, 42, 90 (top) courtesy of Northwestern University; pp. 62, 64, 66, 67 courtesy of D. Y. Begay; p. 78 courtesy of R. C. Gorman gallery.

Contents

Introduction   7

One
Beginnings   11

Two
Invasion, Imprisonment, and Return   19

Three
Current Government   35

Four
Today's Spiritual Beliefs   43

Five
Today's Social Structures   55

Six
Modern Arts   63

Seven
Contributions to the World   75

Eight
Challenges for Today,
Hopes for the Future   85

Further Reading   91
For More Information   92
Glossary   93
Index   95

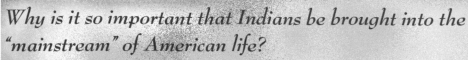

Why is it so important that Indians be brought into the "mainstream" of American life?
I would not know how to interpret this phrase to my people.
The closest I would be able to come would be "a big wide river".
Am I then to tell my people that they are to be thrown into the big, wide river of the United States?

Earl Old Person
Blackfeet Tribal Chairman

Introduction

In the midst of twenty-first-century North America, how do the very first North Americans hold on to their unique cultural identity? At the same time, how do they adjust to the real demands of the modern world? Earl Old Person's quote on the opposite page expresses the difficulty of achieving this balance. Even the common values of the rest of North America—like fitting into the "mainstream"—may seem strange or undesireable to North American Indians. How can these groups of people thrive and prosper in the twenty-first century without losing their traditions, the ways of thinking and living that have been handed down to them by their ancestors? How can they keep from drowning in North America's "big, wide river"?

Thoughts from the Series Consultant

Each of the books in this series was written with the help of Native scholars and tribal leaders from the particular tribe. Based on oral histories as well as written documents, these books describe the current strategies of each Native nation to develop its economy while maintaining strong ties with its culture. As a result, you may find that these books read far differently from other books about Native Americans.

Over the past centuries, Native groups have faced increasing pressure to conform to the wishes of the governments that took their lands. Often brutally inhumane methods were implemented to change Native social systems. These books describe the ways that Native groups refused to be passive recipients of change, even in the face of these past atrocities. Heroic individuals worked to fit external changes into local conditions. This struggle continues today.

The legacy of the past still haunts the psyche of both Native and non-Native people of North America; hopefully, these books will help correct some misunderstandings. And even with the difficulties encountered by past and current Native leaders, Native nations continue to thrive. As this series illustrates, Native populations continue to increase—and they have clearly persevered against incredible odds. North American culture's big, wide river may be deep and cold—but Native Americans are good swimmers!

—*Martha McCollough*

Breaking Stereotypes

One way that some North Americans may "drown" Native culture is by using stereotypes to think about North American Indians. When we use stereotypes to think about a group of people, we assume things about them because of their race or cultural group. Instead of taking time to understand individual differences and situations, we lump together everyone in a certain group. In reality, though, every person is different. More than two million Native people live in North America, and they are as *diverse* as any other group. Each one is unique.

Even if we try hard to avoid stereotypes, however, it isn't always easy to know what words to use. Should we call the people who are native to North America Native Americans—or American Indians—or just Indians?

The word "Indian" probably comes from a mistake—when Christopher Columbus arrived in the New World, he thought he had reached India, so he called the people he found there Indians. Some people feel it doesn't make much sense to call Native Americans "Indians." (Suppose Columbus had thought he landed in China instead of India; would we today call Native people "Chinese"?) Other scholars disagree; for example, Russell Means, Native politician and activist, claims that the word "Indian" comes from Columbus saying the native people were *en Dios*—"in God," or naturally spiritual.

Many Canadians use the term "First Nations" to refer to the Native peoples who live there, and people in the United States usually speak of Native Americans. Most Native people we talked to while we were writing these books prefer the simple term "Indian"—or they would rather use the names of their tribes. (We have used the term "North American Indians" for our series to distinguish this group of people from the inhabitants of India.)

Even the definition of what makes a person "Indian" varies. The U.S. government recognizes certain groups as tribal nations (almost 500 in all). Each nation then decides how it will enroll people as members of that tribe. Tribes may require a particular amount of Indian blood, tribal membership of the father or the mother, or other *criteria*. Some enrolled tribal members who are legally "Indian" may not look Native at all; many have blond hair and blue eyes and others have clearly African features. At the same time, there are thousands of Native people whose tribes have not yet been officially recognized by the government.

We have done our best to write books that are as free from stereotypes as possible. But you as the reader also play a part. After reading one of these books, we hope you won't think: "The Cheyenne are all like this" or "Iroquois are all like that." Each person in this world is unique, whatever their culture. Stereotypes shut people's minds—but these books are intended to open your mind. North American Indians today have much wisdom and beauty to offer.

Some people consider American Indians to be a historical topic only, but Indians today are living, contributing members of North American society. The contributions of the various Indian cultures enrich our world—and North America would be a very different place without the Native people who live there. May they never be lost in North America's "big, wide river"!

Window Rock is located on the Arizona side of the Arizona–New Mexico border. The ceremonial name of this natural rock formation is Ni' 'AlnÍ'gi—Earth's Center. It is also called TséghÁhoodzÁní—Perforated Rock.

Chapter 1

Beginnings

Yáatéeh!
("Welcome!" in the Diné language.)

How can I tell you about the Navajo—the Diné? They are so many, so diverse. They live in the ancient lands they call Dinétah and in modern cities like Gallup and Los Angeles. They are young and old, *traditional* yet *progressive*. They drive SUVs and ride horses. They live in *hoogans* and apartments. They follow the ancient Blessing Way and worship in Christian churches. They play punk rock and haunting traditional wood flute. They are the largest Indian nation and some of America's most patriotic citizens. They walk in beauty even while they struggle against poverty. They have adapted customs from others, yet are still their own unique selves. They are people of rich contradiction. And they are our neighbors, who have much to offer us.

They call themselves *Diné* (pronounced "dee-nay"), which means "the People." The Mexicans called them "Apaches Du Naha." The Navajo and the Apache share the same roots, and the Navajo language is very similar to that of the Apache.

Modern homes and a hoogan share the land in front of a majestic butte near Tsaile, Arizona. Spectacular natural scenery and traditional and modern ways of life all share the same space in Dinétah.

The Navajo Nation has 250,000 enrolled members. This makes them the largest Indian nation in North America. In the 2000 U.S. Census, 300,000 people indicated they were at least part Navajo. Dinétah (Navajo Nation), which includes parts of Arizona, New Mexico, and Utah, covers 27,000 square miles (approximately 69,231 square kilometers). That's larger than ten of the fifty U.S. states. It is a land of incredible beauty.

To understand the Diné we have to begin with their own traditions about their place in the world. The Diné have an account of their Creation, which they regard as sacred truth, much as Christians or Jews regard the Bible story of Creation. This story was not written but handed down through time by living voices. This sacred understanding has similarities to the traditions of the Pueblo Indians, who tell of emerging from underground worlds, and to the Apache, who tell of Changing Woman and Twin Heroes. This suggests ancient connections between these groups of people. More important, it explains the inseparable connection between the Diné people and Dinétah—the lands between the sacred mountains.

According to tradition, Spider Woman first taught Diné women the art of weaving. They have excelled at this art form for centuries. This mural is in the Navajo Nation Council Chambers.

The Diné tell how they came up through a magic reed from three previous underworlds into this fourth "Glittering World." In the other three worlds, people were not like they are today. They were animals, insects, or masked spirits. These are depicted in Navajo ceremonies to this day.

First Man and First Woman were two of the first beings. First Man was made in the east from a joining of white and black clouds. First Woman was made in the west from the joining of yellow and blue clouds. Spider Woman is another ancient being from the first world. She taught Navajo women the art of weaving.

Once they climbed through the lower worlds into this Glittering World, where we live today, people built a *sweat house* and sang the Blessing Song. They constructed the first house (a *hoogan*—usually spelled "hogan" by non-Navajo) exactly as Talking God told them. In this hoogan, the people arranged their world.

They named the four sacred mountains surrounding the land, which serve as the hoogan's foundations. They also established four sacred ma-

Ceremonial dry paintings represent the Holy People, powerful supernatural beings revered by the Navajo.

Spider Woman, who taught the Diné to weave, lived in Canyon De Chelly. When Edward Curtis took this photo of Navajo horsemen in Canyon De Chelly in 1907, it had been the heartland of the Navajo Nation for several centuries.

terials. Mount Blanco (Tsisnaasjini'), in Colorado is the Navajo's eastern foundation and represents the white shell stone. Mount Taylor (Tsoodzil), east of Grants, New Mexico, is the Navajo's southern foundation and represents the turquoise stone. San Francisco Peaks (Dook'o'oslííd), located just north of Flagstaff, is the western foundation; it represents abalone and coral. Mount Hesperus (Dibé Nitsaa) in Colorado, the northern foundation, represents the black jet stone.

The "Holy People" are powerful supernatural beings revered by the Diné. The Holy People put the sun and the moon into the sky. Then they began to place stars in the night in an orderly way. This took a long time and lots of discussion. Coyote had little patience. He seized the corner of the blanket where the Holy People had laid the stars and threw the remaining stars pell-mell, helter-skelter into the sky. After that, the Holy People kept on creating the elements of the world that support life and bring beauty—clouds, trees, and rain.

The Navajo Nation is crossed by highways; it is the largest North American Indian nation today.

All was good and the people were happy. Then, calamity came. Evil monsters appeared and began to kill the Earth People. But a miracle saved them. Ever Changing Woman (Asdzaa Nádleehé) was born at what is now Gobernador Knob, New Mexico. She married the Sun and bore two sons. These twins are heroes to the Navajo people. Their names are "Monster Slayer" and "Child-Born-of-Water."

The twins traveled to their father the Sun and asked for supernatural weapons to fight the dreaded monsters. The Sun gave them lightning bolts. Every time the Hero Twins killed a monster, it turned to stone. Lava flows near Mount Taylor in New Mexico are believed to be blood from the death of Ye'iitsoh, or the "Monster Who Sucked in People." Some angular rock formations in Dinétah, such as the immense Black Mesa (Dzil Yíjiin), are also seen as the stone remains of the monsters.

The Diné tell of people who lived during the monster time—what scientists now call the prehistoric era. These were Water Edge People, Corn People (those who cultivated corn) and Arrow People (those who made the large stone points now called sandia, folsom, and clovis, and who used the spear thrower or atlatl). Over the centuries, clans from other people groups joined with the Diné. The Paiutes came with their beautiful baskets. The Anasazis—who lived in great *adobe* apartment buildings—traded with the Diné. Utes and Apaches also mingled with the people. Over time, the children or grandchildren of these people became Diné.

Changing Woman went to live in the western skies, in a land that was afloat, where she would be close to her husband the sun. Her home was made of the four sacred materials: white shell, turquoise, abalone shell, and black jet. These were associated with the four clans she made from her skin—the Towering House People, Near Water People, Bitter Water People, and Mud People. These newly created clans heard they had relatives in the east and wanted to meet them. They migrated from the western skies to New Mexico. When finally they arrived at Dinétah, they joined the other clans already living there. Together, the Diné lived in *hózhó*—the way of peace, harmony, and good health.

These sacred Creation accounts explain many of the elements that are essential to Diné identity. Although they do not own all their original lands, they are still located between the four sacred mountains. As you will see in the next chapter, they sacrificed much to live there. The hoogan is still the center of ceremonial life—and many Diné still live in hoogans today. Clans are an important social structure. The modern Navajo people live in many places and many ways . . . and they continue to live in hózhó.

Canyon del Muerto, which means "Canyon of the Dead." In 1805, Lt. Antonio Narbona, later the governor of the Province of New Mexico, led a Spanish expedition in an all-day battle with a band of Navajos fortified in a rock shelter in Canyon del Muerto. At the end of the day, Narbona's contingent had killed 105 Navajos. Sixty years later, Kit Carson led American troops in a campaign to kill, starve, and subjugate Navajos in Canyon De Chelly. Today, the rock shelter is called Massacre Cave.

Chapter 2

Invasion, Imprisonment, and Return

Navajo Nation is a great place to visit. People are friendly. There are incredible sights to see. Monument Valley, Canyon De Chelly and Rainbow Rock are awesome spectacles. But if you ever travel to the Navajo's land, remember: the Diné made great sacrifices to be where they are today. The survival of the Diné is a story of invasion, imprisonment, and finally, a return to their land.

Archaeologists studying ancient remains have tried to reconstruct Navajo roots. Until recently, many historians believed that the Navajo and Apaches came from northwestern Canada to the southwest United States just five hundred years ago. This was based on similarities between the Athapascan languages of Navajo and Arctic Native peoples. The name Athapascan comes from Lake Athabasca in northern Canada. The mother language of the Athapascan is Na-Dene, a language that branched out to

"Those called sheep are your mother; sheep are your life"—Old Diné saying. Edward Curtis took this picture of Navajo herds before the reduction of Navajo sheep by the federal government in the 1930s.

Northern, Northern Pacific, and Southwest regions of North America. The Navajo, however, do not agree that their ancestors came from the north; instead, they tell of a group that left them and traveled north—the opposite of archaeologists' theories.

Navajo spoken history tells of clans that began in the Southwest in very ancient times and other clans that came to join them from the Pacific Coast. Recent scholarly research supports these traditions. Navajo historian AnCita Benally points to similarities between Navajo and the language of the Hupa Indians in California. The latest archeological evidence also supports the Navajo's belief that they lived on their land long before what archeologists once believed; Dr. Andrew E. Douglass has found the remains of Navajo hoogans dating from A.D. 1000 in the Southwest.

The arrival of the Spanish in North America introduced significant changes to the Diné way of life—horses, sheep, and deadly warfare. The Diné lived a more settled way of life than the *nomadic* Apaches and Comanches, but they appreciated the benefits of horses for hunting and transportation. Navajo have long been noted for their skills as horsemen and continue to enjoy riding and rodeo.

Sheep also became a huge part of Diné cultural identity. The Navajo acquired large herds, which provided mutton for food and wool for weaving. Sheepherding became connected to security, identity, and social organization. An old Diné saying was: "Those called sheep are your mother; sheep are life."

Europeans also brought warfare and slavery. More than any other group of North American Indians, the Diné were raided by the Spanish to supply slaves for their ranches. Spanish governors took advantage of the Navajo's peaceful ways and became rich kidnapping and selling Indian slaves on a large scale.

The Diné may have loved peace, but they were not *pacifists*. They would not allow the Spanish to wipe them out. Fighting back, the Diné raided Spanish settlements for horses and livestock.

Canyon De Chelly offered protection with its towering *mesas* and many enclosures. By 1700, this area had become the heart of Dinétah. Orchards provided fruit, fields yielded corn, and there was grass for the sheep to graze and water for all.

Relations changed between the Diné and nearby Pueblo Indians. In some cases, the Spanish settled among the Pueblos, and so Navajo warfare against the Spaniards involved other Indians as well. At the same time, members of other *indigenous* nations settled among the Diné. Over the years, Latinos and people of African descent also joined themselves to the Navajo.

Warfare was not the only way the Spanish and Navajo related to each other; at times they traded. In the early 1800s, Diné culture profited from Mexican craft ideas. Spanish *vaqueros* (cowboys) wore fancy silver decorations on their clothing, and these silver designs inspired Navajo craftsmen to begin the artistic silver work for which they are famous. The Spanish also had brightly colored dyes for cloth, and the Diné incorporated bright colors into their intricate weaving designs.

In 1846, the United States took control of New Mexico and Arizona from Mexico. America's worst *atrocities* against the Diné were committed early in the 1860s. Mexicans were continuing to raid from the south for slaves, and the Navajo were continuing to fight back, so the U.S. Army was sent to subdue the Diné. This was supposedly as punishment for the Navajo raids against the Mexicans, but there is more to the story. American commander James H. Carlton had written his Washington superiors that "fields of gold and other precious minerals" lay beneath Navajo lands. If the Navajo were gone, then these could be mined and sold to raise money for "the war against slavery," which was then being fought.

In 1863, Christopher "Kit" Carson was chosen to lead a campaign of *extermination* or removal against the Navajo. With a thousand troops and Indian scouts, Carson laid the Dinétah to waste. Fields were burned, orchards hacked down, wells poisoned—and the fleeing Diné starved. Carson pursued them into Canyon De Chelly. Some Western Navajo man-

"First Woman, when she was created, gave us this piece of land and created it especially for us and gave us the whitest of corn."—Barboncito, Diné leader, in 1868. This mural in the Navajo Nation Council Chamber shows Diné women grinding corn using stone tools.

This mural in the Navajo Nation's council chambers portrays the forced march from Canyon De Chelly to Bosque Redondo.

aged to evade the troops and stay in the land. Most, however, were forced to undertake what has been called "the Long Walk."

Some eight thousand people, already half starved and exhausted from the Carson campaign, were forced to trudge three hundred miles (about 483 kilometers). A spoken account by Navajo Gus Bighorse told what it was like:

> The trip is on foot. People are shot on the spot if they say they are tired or sick or if they stop to help someone. If a woman is in labor with a baby, she is killed. Many get sick and get diarrhea because of the food. They are heartbroken because their families die on the way.

Invasion, Imprisonment, and Return   23

Thanks to assertive and wise leadership, the Navajo were allowed to leave the desolate conditions at Bosque Redondo and return to Dinétah. This portion of the mural at the Navajo Nation's council chambers portrays the signing of the treaty allowing their return.

Their destination was Fort Sumner at Bosque Redondo. The Diné call it *Hweeldi*—a term derived from the Spanish word for "fort." Imprisonment there was a nightmare. The ground was unsuited for farming, and the water was undrinkable. Flour, supplied by the government, consisted in large part of slate and plaster of paris—a trick to save money by dishonest government traders. The Diné died from illnesses, starvation, attacks by Comanches, and from wolves that stole into their camp and preyed on those too weak to defend themselves.

In 1868, Barboncito and other Navajo leaders were taken to Washington. Barboncito talked to everyone he could about the Navajo's dilemma at Fort Sumner. He made it clear to anyone who would listen that the prisoners would rebel if a solution to this intolerable situation were not found.

The U.S. government sent General Sherman to Bosque Redondo to find another place for the Navajo. Barboncito told Sherman that the Navajo were in the wrong place: "Our grandfathers had no idea of living in any other country except our own. When the Navajo were first created, four mountains . . . were pointed out to us . . . that was to be our country." Barboncito concluded his remarks by saying: "I hope to God you will not ask me to go to any other country than my own. It might turn out to be another Bosque Redondo."

A new treaty was signed on June 1, 1868. It allowed the Diné to return to a portion of their homeland. The people finally walked back to their homeland; when Mount Taylor came into view, they sat down and cried. Many hardships were still ahead of them, but they felt sure they could survive once they were back home in Dinétah.

Sheepherding continued to provide a livelihood for most Navajo. In the late 1800s, a market opened up for Navajo rugs. The Diné had long been known for their weaving, and now, as railroads reached the far West, Navajo weaving could be more affordably sent for sale in the East. The telegraph also made it easier to communicate orders and sales.

Don Lorenzo Hubbell set up his trading post in 1876 on Navajo land in Ganado, Arizona. The Diné brought their handmade artwork there and exchanged them for lamps, oil, saddles, sugar, cloth, and other needed items. The demand for Navajo crafts enabled Hubbell to prosper. He and his sons eventually owned thirty trading posts, wholesale businesses in Gallup and Winslow, and stagecoach and freight lines. Hubbell explained: "The first duty of an Indian trader is to look after the material welfare of his neigh-

Beginning in 1876, Hubbell's trading post was an important part of the Navajo economy. Don Lorenzo Hubbell believed that if he prospered, the Navajo would too.

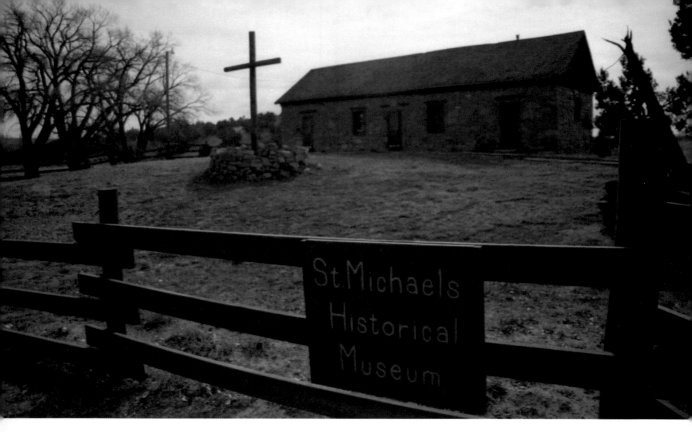

In 1898, Franciscan Fathers arrived on the Navajo reservation and began the first Christian mission there. This is the original building of St. Michael's Mission, now a museum.

bors; to advise them to produce that which their natural talent best adapts to; to treat them honestly."

The 1890s saw new threats to Navajo land holdings. The reservation given them was only ten percent of their original territory, and white ranchers and **prospectors** kept moving onto Navajo land. The U.S. federal government repeatedly pushed for the Navajo reservation to be "apportioned." This would give each family a small lot. Private Navajo owners would then be allowed to sell their land. Such policies were a way to take Indian lands, since Native landowners were often in poverty and likely to sell. Some tribes lost most of their land in this way. Father Anselm Weber, a **Franciscan friar** at St. Michael's Mission in Arizona, worked ceaselessly opposing allotment. Over the years since then, the Diné have sought to expand their land by purchase and by legal decisions.

Indian Agency schools were another kind of threat to Navajo culture at this time. Most of these were boarding schools. Children were taken—some literally kidnapped—from their homes to the schools. Conditions were awful at the schools. Students were poorly fed, clothed, and sheltered. Many died from illnesses. Any evidence of Navajo language, customs, and culture was severely punished. Many Navajo still alive today regret the years of school that separated them from their families and culture.

Then, in 1922, oil was discovered in Dinétah. The **Bureau of Indian Affairs** encouraged the Diné to form the Navajo Business Council, which would have authority to represent the tribe in making contracts with oil developers. Henry Chee Dodge was one of the most important members of this new council, a man who continued to have strong influence in his people's struggles through the early twentieth century. The Navajo Business Council was an important step toward the Dinés' concept of themselves as a nation.

In the 1930s, the Diné had a new factor to deal with—John Collier, the new head of federal Indian policies. Some tribes remember Collier favorably, since he reversed the government's attempts to wipe out Indian

In 1922, oil was found on the Navajo Nation.

There were great changes in federal Indian policy in the 1930s. The head of the Bureau of Indian Affairs, John Collier, urged Indian nations to form modern governments. He also ordered that overgrazing sheep be killed.

languages and customs. The Navajo, however, encountered a more negative aspect of his administration.

Despite continuous efforts to attain land, the Navajo Nation in the 1930s was not increasing fast enough to support their flocks of sheep. Collier and other federal **bureaucrats** decided the herds would have to be decreased. They hired men to come onto Navajo lands and shoot countless sheep. Since there was no market for mutton during the *Great Depression*, the carcasses were left to rot or burned in pits. A Diné woman remembers:

"Our people cried. My people, they cried." For people whose culture and livelihood depended on sheep, it was a harsh blow.

Despite the way the U.S. government had treated them, the Diné responded valiantly in 1941 when Pearl Harbor was bombed and Uncle Sam called for help in the war. About 3,600 Navajo men and twelve Navajo women served in the American Armed Services. Many of them walked long distances or hitchhiked in order to enlist. They earned recognition for their abilities and courage in wartime. Years later, a Navajo man was asked why he volunteered to fight in "a white man's war." He replied: "We are proud to be Americans. We are proud to be American Indians. We always stand ready when our country needs us."

When they returned from the war, Navajo servicemen were angry that they still could not vote. Indian servicemen asked: "If we risked our lives to defend this country, why are we not treated as citizens?" Finally, in 1924, the federal government gave Native Americans the right to vote in national

---

Important Terms

Athapascan
A family of languages. Navajo, Apache, Hupa, and certain Arctic groups are Athapascan languages. Navajo and Apache are very similar, and Navajo is also considered an Apache language.

Canyon De Chelly
A beautiful area of mesas and ravines in Arizona. Ancient cliff dwellers left impressive villages in the caves located there. Canyon De Chelly was the heart of Dinétah from the 1700s to 1863 and is still part of the Navajo Nation.

Bosque Redondo
Hweeldi
Fort Sumner
These are all names for the same place—where the Diné were kept captive from 1863 to 1868.

Some 3,600 Navajo men and twelve women served in World War II. The most famous were the Code Talkers. This larger than life-size bronze statue by renowned Ute-Navajo Indian sculptor Oreland Joe is in the Southwest Indian Foundation Cultural Center in Gallup, New Mexico.

elections; states did not grant them the same privilege. Arizona at last gave American Indians the right to vote in 1948; New Mexico followed suit in 1953, and Utah in 1957.

The end of the Second World War brought the start of the Atomic Age—and in 1951, *uranium* was discovered on Navajo Land. Mining operations rushed in, and jobs were offered to Diné workers. The companies did not provide safe working conditions, however, and workers came home with dangerous uranium dust on their clothes. The daughter of a uranium mine worker remembers how her family once found a mouse that had settled into her father's discarded work clothes and died overnight.

In 1962, the U.S. government made a crucial decision in a conflict over land between the Navajo and the Hopi. The land dispute had been going on for almost a century before then and continues more than forty years after. The issue is complex, heated, and perceived quite differently by the two tribes. The 1962 ruling created a "joint use area," with a governing panel consisting of members from both tribes. It was an ineffective solution. A later ruling required more than ten thousand Navajo to leave their homes in return for cash settlements. The issue is still not fully settled.

Peabody Coal signed a thirty-five-year lease in 1966, which was expected to bring in two million dollars a year for the tribe. The coal mining operation would be in the Black Mesa area, property belonging to both Navajo and Hopi nations. Many members of both tribes were unaware that the lease involved water rights as well as coal rights. An underground pipeline used more than a billion gallons (about 3.8 billion liters) of water a year to push coal 275 miles (about 440 kilometers). By 1972, it was obvious that the water on Navajo lands was being drained away.

In 1969, a resolution passed that the Diné be officially known as "the Navajo Nation." The same year saw the establishment of Diné College, the first college established and maintained by an Indian nation.

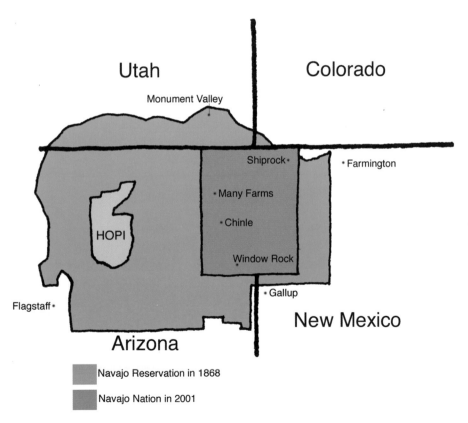

This map shows the boundaries of the Navajo reservation in 1868 and today.

Peter MacDonald was elected as chairman of the Navajo Nation in 1971. He was a strong and gifted communicator, liked by young and old members of the Nation. When outsiders threatened Navajo interests, he played political hardball. He gained Navajo control over schools on Navajo land, and he fought against Peabody Coal.

In July 1979, the largest nuclear accident in U.S. history devastated the Churchrock Diné community. United Nuclear Corporation's dam broke at a uranium mill holding pond and poured a hundred million gallons (380 million liters) of *radioactive* water into the Río Puerco River. Unlike the accident three months earlier at the Three Mile Island Nuclear Power Plant in Pennsylvania, the spill went unnoticed by the American media. Residents continue to fear the effects of contamination from the spill.

Ten years later would be a tumultuous time for the Navajo Nation. Despite Peter MacDonald's long and popular political career, the Navajo council removed him from office in 1989 after he was involved in a financial scandal. A demonstration between supporters and foes of MacDonald ended in two tragic deaths. In 1991, MacDonald was sent to federal prison on charges related to the riot.

In 1996, an Arizona federal judge ruled against Peabody Coal Company, America's largest coal producer, in favor of the Diné living in Black Mesa. The judge denied the company an operating permit, because Peabody's strip mine polluted the air, contaminated groundwater, affected the health

Mining operations have brought significant amounts of money to the Navajo Nation, but also controversy over environmental damage.

Today, there are 250,000 enrolled members of the Navajo tribe, most of whom live on Navajo Nation lands in Arizona and New Mexico.

of Indians in the area, killed their sheep, and destroyed Indian burial sites. The suit was initiated by the Diné Alliance, a Navajo organization of more than five hundred Navajo from Black Mesa.

The political and environmental struggles of recent years may seem far removed from the battles the Navajo fought against Mexican slavers and Kit Carson, but they share a common theme. If the Navajo are to thrive and maintain traditional ways in their own land, they still must confront challenges with determination and courage.

Navajo Council Chambers in Window Rock Arizona are the political heart of the Navajo Nation. The flags are flown only when the council is in session.

Chapter 3

Current Government

J oe Shirley has plenty of challenges ahead of him. At the start of 2003, he was the newly elected president of the Navajo Nation, America's largest Indian Nation both in membership and in land mass. One of his first priorities is education. He has a bachelor's degree in business and a master's degree in social work, so he knows the value of academic success. He wants to see academic standards for Diné schools come "up to par" as he puts it. He also wants to see guaranteed student loans for Diné scholars and support services to improve their chances of success in college.

At the same time, President Shirley needs to work on ways for the Navajo culture to be strengthened. Shirley would like to see a program to fund the work of *medicine men* and *apprentices*. Medicine men are often poor, and few young people can afford to spend years apprenticed to elder healers in order to continue this sacred calling. President Shirley is also concerned about ways to keep the Diné language in vital use among young people.

Unemployment is another big issue facing the new president. Half the workers in Navajo Nation are unemployed, and many young people leave

Ray Ashley is proud to work at the Navajo Nation government offices.

the reservation to find work elsewhere. Shirley hopes to develop ways for businesses to get started more easily in the Navajo Nation. Alcohol and drug abuse must also be addressed, as these cause considerable suffering among the Diné. And improvement of the nation's ***infrastrucure*** is also needed; many homes lack electric power or telephone lines, and roads often become impassible in rough weather.

Of course, none of this is up to the president alone. The majority of the tribal council are newly elected members. Diné voters sent a clear signal that they were unhappy with the former council. Now, the new representatives have to prove that they can do the job—working for the people rather than for their own interests, seeing results, and maintaining high ethical standards. As Joe Shirley put it when he was announced the election winner: "The real work begins now."

As sovereign nations within the borders of the United States, each Indian nation has the authority to choose its own leaders and make its own laws, providing these do not interfere with the laws and business of the U.S. federal government. Councils of Indian Nations today have great power and responsibility in their communities. They protect land and water rights. They negotiate with other governments. They make laws. They watch over businesses and charitable organizations. In short, they are involved in almost every major matter within tribal borders.

The origins of today's Diné tribal council go back to the oil deals of the 1920s, when the Navajo Business Council was formed. At that time, the U.S. government appointed representatives. During the 1930s, a tribal council was created with twelve representatives. In 1991, the Navajo Nation Council was created in its present form.

The Navajo Nation Code established three branches of government, like the U.S. government. The president and vice president form the executive branch, and the court is the judiciary branch. The legislative branch consists of the Navajo Nation Council and any groups formed under the council. Eighty-eight council delegates represent 110 chapters or communities. Navajo women are increasingly involved in politics; ten women are on the 2003 council. The eighty-eight delegates are divided into twelve standing committees, which is where the majority of the council's work is done. When discussing legislation, representatives speak the Diné language—a

Navajo Nation tribal government offices are built in the midst of natural rock formations, giving them a sense of beauty and grandeur.

The Great Seal of the Navajo Nation shows the four sacred mountains that border Dinétah, and livestock that have traditionally been so important to Navajo life.

good example of how the Navajo are progressive while retaining their culture.

The Navajo Nation Council chambers, designed by architect Jim Nailer, are visually impressive. The office complex is set among enormous red rock formations within sight of the monumental Window Rock formation. Viewed from the outside, the bottom half of the building resembles a kiva—a ceremonial sacred chamber. The top half looks like a hoogan. Inside, the chambers are surrounded by murals depicting Diné history—from before the arrival of the Europeans to today.

The Navajo Nation Council is the largest and most complex system of Native American government in the United States. Other tribes around the country seek their endorsement when bringing issues before the national government. The council is also a model for other nations; indigenous people from around the world have visited Window Rock to learn how the Navajo government works. The Diné are rightly proud of their governmental system.

In January of 2000, the Navajo Nation made significant changes in its criminal code. The council eliminated jail time for seventy-nine offenses, requiring instead the use of peacemakers in court cases. This put into the court system the traditional Diné practice of *nalyeeh*—confronting someone who hurts others with a demand for communication . . . so something positive will come from the original damage. This mediation process brings together the person accused of a crime with the person and family he or she harmed. A court appointed "peacemaker" moderates the discussion. The peacemaker plays the traditional role of the *naat'aani*, a leader whose success depends on earned respect and powers of persuasion. The parties talk about what happened and form a plan to set things right again.

Chief Justice Robert Yazzie is quoted in Peter Iverson's book *Diné*:

The prison approach to crime does not work. Western **adjudication** is the search for what happened and who did it; Navajo peacemaking is about the effects of what happened. Who got hurt? What do they feel about it? What can be done to repair the harm?

Alcohol is a factor in many Diné legal cases. The accused must deal with what the Diné call *maaye'e'*—"the monster within" of alcoholism. He or she must also deal with the person he has harmed. The offender makes restitution, payment for the harm he or she has done. This might involve giving a favorite piece of jewelry or a prized horse to the injured party.

Judge Yazzie concludes:

We know that peacemaking works. It has proven successful in problem areas such as driving while intoxicated, delinquency, family violence, and alcohol-related crime. It allows families to be involved in helping their relatives (whether they are the ones doing the hurting or the ones who got hurt), and it helps everyone look at the monster of what happened and its effects.

The process is emotional. Judge Yazzie says the most important paperwork in peacemaking are the tissues used to dry tears. The final goal of the peacemaking process is a restoration to hózhó—peace, harmony, and positive outcomes—for all parties.

The Navajo government is the largest employer on the nation. The various departments oversee numerous programs for public health and maintenance of their lands. One example is the Navajo Veterinary Program.

Tova Salaybe works for the Navajo Veterinary Program.

The Navajo Veterinary Program stays busy traveling from town to town in Dinétah with a mobile unit, **spaying** and **neutering** up to twenty-five animals a day. This service is valuable for Diné pet owners, since many people in the nation lack electricity, the roads are unpaved, and some people lack transportation.

Tova Salabye is a young Diné woman working with the Navajo Veterinary Program. She is the Community Outreach Coordinator for SNAP (Spay and Neuter Program) at the Window Rock Veterinary Clinic. Tova lives on the Navajo Nation in Nazalini, Arizona. She grew up loving animals and has many dogs, cats, and sheep. She speaks at schools, chapter houses (meeting places for local government chapters), and on the radio. She also writes newspaper articles in Diné and English.

It has not been easy for the Diné to develop a governmental system that will meet the needs of their large nation. In many cases, leaders have used trial and error to find what works best, and this process has worked better at some times than at others. Thanks to talented leadership and *perseverance*, however, they have achieved today's Navajo government system. By combining modern governmental forms and traditional lifeways, the Diné have developed a government that serves their own needs and offers a model to other communities as well.

In 1907, Edward Curtis photographed this Hataali—what people commonly call a "medicine man." Today, there are still young Navajo men training to continue the ceremonies for healing.

Chapter 4

Today's Spiritual Beliefs

"Having that first drink, it's just like lighting a fire." The words are those of a noted Diné silversmith quoted in an article by Leslie Linthicum in the *Gallup Independent*. He isn't the only person in Dinétah struggling with alcohol. Drinking alcohol is not permitted on Navajo lands, but Gallup borders the Navajo Nation; people go there to buy booze.

Not too long ago, 40,000 people a year were admitted to the Gallup jail on charges of intoxication. Most of these charges were issued to the same people—a core group of seven hundred, many of whom spent the majority of their lives in short stays at the jail. They'd sober up in jail, get referred to alcoholism counseling, and be released. The silversmith quoted above is typical of this group; he tried Alcoholics Anonymous and other programs, but he still could not shake off what the Diné call Naayée—"the monster" of alcoholic illness.

All Navajo ceremonies require dry painting, commonly called "sandpainting."

Now, however, he and many others have found help that works. It isn't modern medicine or psychology that provides the solution. It's a program that relies on traditional Diné beliefs to achieve sobriety and hózhó. The Na'Nizhoozhi Center is the largest **detoxification** center in the nation—and one of the least expensive. Their most successful program is Hin-n'ah Bits'os or "Eagle Plume." Harrison Jim, a Road Man (spiritual guide) of the Native American Church and a Diné healer, is one of the cofounders. He is also a recovering alcoholic. After studying modern, scientific approaches to alcoholism, he found that Diné spirituality was the strongest medicine for the illness.

The program uses four sweat lodges and four hoogans. Counselors introduce themselves in the traditional Diné way—by their clan identities. Instead of calling the people receiving treatment "clients," they are addressed as "relatives." Healing involves sweats, burning cedar bark, drumming and chanting, singing, and discussing the teachings of the Holy People.

The Eagle Plume program is remarkably effective, reducing the rate of intoxication arrests in Gallup and enabling Diné men to reclaim control of their lives. One "relative" in the program, a sandpainter, explains: "Somewhere along the way, I made mistakes. I am learning to bring myself back into harmony."

It's not surprising that traditional ways provide the best help for Diné men in recovery. The Navajo people are noted for spirituality. However, the Diné do not have a "religion" as non-Indians use the term. There is no word for religion in the Diné language. Raymond Friday Locke explains:

> The Navajo's concept of religion is so total that it can be said that there is no such thing as religion in Navajo culture because everything is religious. Everything a Navajo knows—his shelter, his fields, his livestock, the sky above him, and the ground on which he walks—is holy.

A Navajo man named Ray Ashley says: "The Navajo see holiness in all of life all around." The Diné have no large building for worship equivalent

Almost all the Southwest Indians use dry painting for healing rituals, but none have developed it to such beauty and complexity as the Diné sandpainting.

Saint Michael's Catholic Mission, in St. Michael's, Arizona, on the Navajo Nation, has been a part of Navajo life for more than a century.

to Christian church or Jewish synagogue. There is no calendar pattern for worship. As Raymond Friday Locke said:

> Religious rites and practices are an essential element in nearly every aspect of traditional Navajo culture, pervading it to such an extent that . . . it was several decades before white Americans living among the Navajo realized they possessed any form of worship at all.

The *Diyinii*—a Diné word that means "particular ones who are holy"— are important for Diné life and culture. The Holy People are also called *Diyin Diné*; these were the first beings in the world beneath this one. The Diyinii are not holy in the sense of being morally upright, as they may experience jealousy, anger, and fear; yet they are connected to Creation's health and wholeness. They cannot be seen in their actual forms since parting from the Earth Surface People. They are seen as natural objects and phenomenon such as wind or corn. Healing ceremonies bring people into contact with these supernatural beings, thus restoring people to health.

The Navajo do not distinguish one supernatural being as a Supreme

Important Terms

sweat lodge
A small hoogan in which stones and water produce heat and steam. Sweats are used for spiritual communion and purifying the body.

Diyinii
"Holy People," supernatural beings who influence the lives of ordinary mortals, and whose power is drawn upon in healing ceremonies.

Hataali
A person who conducts healing ceremonies and who sings the complicated songs required for healing. Commonly called a "medicine man" by whites.

dry painting
More commonly called sandpainting. Tiny grains of natural substances form a picture, which is created and then destroyed on the hoogan floor in Diné ceremonies. Non-sacred sandpaintings are now a commercial art form.

Native American Church
A spiritual faith combining elements of Christian belief and Native customs from a variety of tribes. Sometimes referred to as "peyotists" due to the ceremonial use of the peyote cactus.

Franciscan
A religious order of the Roman Catholic Church, begun by St. Francis of Assisi. Franciscans are noted for charity and reverence for nature.

The Diyin Shich'ááNn naagháii Prayer Chapel at Saint Michael's Catholic Mission is built in the shape of a hoogan.

Inside the prayer chapel is a sculpture by German artist Ludwig Schumacher, sculpted from a single 500-year-old juniper tree. The carving was given in 1992, in the hopes that the chapel and sculpture might help to heal the 500-year-old wounds left when Europeans came to the Americas.

Being. Instead, there are several important supernatural beings: Changing Woman (Estsa'natlehi), her sons the Hero Twins, Sun, First Man, and First Woman. There are also beings called Helpers, who bridge the gap between the Holy People and the Earth Surface People.

The Diné work for a state of balance in the universe, keeping helpful and destructive forces in harmony. Ceremonials, also called "Sings" or "Ways," are used to keep the Diné in harmony with the forces around them. There are fifty-eight Ways, each with variations, and a hundred books like this one would be needed to describe them all in detail.

A *hataali*—a singer, chanter, or medicine man—conducts incredibly complex ceremonies. The Night Way, for example, has 576 songs. Each song must be sung—word for word—with perfect intonation. A long ceremony may last nine days. In addition to the songs, the hataali must also see that symbols, dances, and dry painting are done perfectly. The Diné believe

Today Baptists, Pentecostals, Seventh Day Adventists, and Mormons have churches in Navajo Nation, along with Catholics and the Native American Church.

that real harm can result for participants if ceremonies are performed incorrectly. For these reasons, each hataali is highly specialized, learning only two or three ceremonies.

Ceremonies may be needed to restore harmony caused by illness, tragedy, distress, or natural disaster. The most serious affliction is witchcraft. *Divination* by hand trembling, stargazing, or listening is used to determine what has caused disharmony and what Way must be conducted to restore balance.

Curing Ways are associated with specific afflictions. Illnesses caused by cold or rain require the Hailway and Waterway ceremonies. Injuries received from lightning strikes are healed by the Shooting Chant. The Windway and Beautyway are used for snakebite. The Beautyway also addresses aches in the body and confusion. Paralysis or psychotic illness, which is uncommon among the Diné, requires the Night Chant.

All ceremonies require dry painting (more commonly—but less correctly—called "sandpainting"). Although dry painting is used in healing rituals by almost all Indians of the Southwest, none have developed it to such beauty and complexity as the Diné. Ceremonies involve dozens of different dry paintings for each occasion. Almost a thousand distinct sandpaintings cover all aspects of Diné life. The Navajo believe that the person who is in a state of disharmony becomes identified with the supernatural beings

Beautyway Song

Today I will walk out
Today everything evil
Will leave me,
I will be as I was before,
I will have a cool breeze
Over my body,
I will walk with a light body,
I will be happy forever,
Nothing will hinder me!

From the Diné Beautyway Ceremony.

portrayed in the dry painting, absorbing power and receiving healing. Each dry painting must be started, finished, and destroyed within a twelve-hour period. At the end of a ceremony, the sands from the painting are gathered in a blanket and scattered to the directions from which they came—east, south, west, north, and then *ni'alnii'* (toward the earth's center) and skyward.

Sometimes earthward and skyward refer to the South Pole and North Pole, or to the Hero Twins. After they rid the earth of the monsters, each twin took a pole for his place. Monster Slayer took the North Pole and assumed the responsibility for **fertility**, **germination**, and growth of life. Child of Water went to the South Pole to be in charge of precipitation. He sends El Niño and La Niña to play a part in the weather of America. Sandpaintings for commercial or artistic purposes are different from those used in Curing Ways.

Many Navajo follow distinct Diné beliefs, but many others choose to worship in the ways offered by the Native American Church (NAC). The NAC is a "Pan-Indian" movement, which means that it combines the beliefs of many different North American Indian tribes. The Navajo Council has opposed the NAC at times, but recently the Council has become more supportive of the church. The NAC now has two buildings in Navajo Nation.

Spiritual life, whether traditional or Christian, gives hope to the Navajo people.

Although it is called a church, the Native American Church does not promote the beliefs of any particular Christian group. It combines traditional American Indian symbolism with Christian beliefs. The Native American Church uses peyote, a small, spineless cactus, as a *sacramental* substance, similar to the way wine is used in Christian ritual. The church teaches strict morality. Members must not drink alcohol, must be faithful to their spouses, and must be honest and nonviolent. Witchcraft and any form of magical arts are utterly forbidden.

For centuries, the Diné were not influenced by Christianity. Efforts to wipe the Navajo out—first by Spaniards, then by Anglo Americans—did not make the newcomers' religion seem attractive to the Diné. At the end of the nineteenth century, however, Mother Katharine Drexel, a Catholic nun whose life was devoted to charitable work among Native American and African American people, persuaded church workers to begin a mission with the Navajo.

In 1898, three men in long robes arrived in Dinétah. The Diné called them *Ednishodi*, "the ones whose clothes drag along." Their Anglo names were Fathers Juvenal and Anselm and Brother Placid, and they were members of the Franciscan Order of the Catholic Church. The Franciscans and Diné were a good spiritual fit, since St. Francis who founded the Franciscan order *revered* nature. He spoke of "Our Sister, Mother Earth," a sentiment with which the Diné could identify.

The Franciscan missionaries began their work in a valley called Ts'ohootso, now known as St. Michael's. They began with learning the Diné language. By 1912, they had produced a two-volume dictionary of the Navajo language. With the encouragement of the Diné, they began St. Michael's School and a health center. Father Anselm opposed government plans to take away Diné land. His continual efforts surveying land, writing government officials, and traveling to Washington D.C. on behalf of the Navajo resulted in more than a million acres (approximately 405,000 hectares) being added to the Navajo lands by the time of his death.

A Mohawk Indian, Kateri Tekakwitha, who lived in upstate New York in the seventeenth century, is revered by Navajo Catholics. The Catholic Church honors her as the patroness of ecology and the environment. When Kateri was eighteen, a French Catholic missionary came to her village and baptized her. She died of an illness at age twenty-four. Her last words were, "Jesus, I love you." Catholics refer to her as "the Lily of the Mohawks," and she was beatified (one step short of being declared a saint) in 1980 by Pope John Paul II. Catholic Indians all over America seek her help through prayer. As Victoria Blair wrote in *Padrea Trail*: "Here among the sage and pinon trees on the vast Navajo Reservation, a Lily grows in the midst of the beautiful mountains. The Lily of the Mohawks is here with the peoples of the Southwest."

In recent years, other Christian churches have been established in Dinétah. Navajo today may worship as Baptists, Pentecostals, Seventh Day Adventists, or Mormons. Others follow the Native American Church, the Catholic Church, or traditional Diné ways.

Shaunda Mae Tsosie, 23, of Chinle, Arizona, is Miss Navajo for 2002–2003.

Chapter 5

Today's Social Structures

"When you grow up, you think back and remember the smells, the fire crackling, the warmth, and the sense of well-being. The hoogan is a rich place full of family, stories, laughter, tragedies, and ceremonies." That is how one Diné park ranger remembers childhood in a hoogan, recounted in the book *The Hogan: the Traditional Navajo Home*.

Driving through the Navajo Nation, one of the most obvious signs of distinctive Diné culture are the hoogans that can be seen from the road. These are unique structures, made with six or eight sides and a doorway facing east. In the past, almost all the Diné lived in these structures. Now, some still use hoogans for their primary residence, but most live in frame houses or manufactured homes, with a hoogan on their property for ceremonial uses.

Hoogans are not only buildings; they represent the Diné way of life. The

Hoogans are not only residences; they also express the Diné way of life.

Navajo Nation Council chambers, the main offices of Diné College, the Prayer Chapel at St. Michael's, the Seventh Day Adventist Church, and even the Subway restaurant in the Navajo Nation are all built in the shape of a hoogan. Diné College is truly a hoogan at heart; in the center of the bottom story is a woodstove and dirt floor, both features of traditional hoogans.

The word *hoogan* literally translates "place home." Traditionally, hoogans are made of logs covered with earth. The oldest hoogans were made with logs piled in a cone shape, somewhat resembling a tepee, then covered with mud. These are termed "male" hoogans and are rarely seen today. More common are six- or eight-sided hoogans, known as "female" style.

Hoogans used to be made from logs covered with dirt for insulation. These provided solid shelter against the extremes of heat and cold that are common in Dinétah. The earthen dome roof represented the sky, and the dirt floor was the earth. A woodstove in the center of the hoogan provided heat and cooking space. The chimney protruded through the center of the building, carrying the smoke away from the interior.

Nowadays, hoogans may be made in the traditional shape from modern materials. They may have concrete or wooden sides, or be made of fitted and uncovered logs. Windows are sometimes added. Tin may be used for roofing.

The cultural importance of the hoogan cannot be overestimated. It is the place for births and weddings, for the ceremony that marks a woman's transition into womanhood, and for healing ceremonies. Small hoogans serve as sweat lodges. According to sacred tradition, First Man and First Woman built the original hoogan, which served as the model for all others. In *The Hoogan: the Traditional Navajo Home*, **anthropologist** John Farella explains:

> The Hoogan is the first thing created, but with the Hoogan one literally creates the universe. All knowledge is contained within that structure. It's a master encoding, a place to begin to understand the Navajo worldview. When you talk to the Navajos, they'll tell you, "Everything I know is here in this Hoogan."

The main poles of each hoogan symbolize the four sacred mountains, the borders of Dinétah, as well as the sacred elements associated with each direction (see chapter one). The poles support the hoogan roof as the

Today, many Navajos live in frame houses, and there are several apartment complexes on the Navajo Nation.

Today's Social Structures 57

four sacred mountains support the sky. The fire in the center of the dwelling represents the North Star, the star that remains unmoving through the seasons and denotes stability in life. When a baby is born, the mother turns its face toward the fire in the center of the hoogan, directing the child toward home and family throughout life. When Diné speak of their home, they say: "That's where my fire is."

The Navajo are matrilineal, which means their primary family identification comes through the women. In a Diné family, the mother is traditionally the most important person. When a couple marries, the husband joins the wife's family. The women have the right to inherit their family's land, house, and livestock. Men own horses, income from their work, and any property they own at the time of marriage. Navajo men are traditionally not allowed to talk with their mothers-in-law. In fact, sons-in-law and mothers-in-law are not supposed to even be in each other's presence. This helps avoid arguments!

Each family is also part of a larger clan. If the hoogan gives physical shape to Navajo culture, clans give relational shape. When Diné introduce themselves, they do so by clans rather than by first name. They first say

The swap meet in Window Rock is an opportunity for Navajos to buy and sell everything from kitchenware to auto parts. It is also a place where Diné artists sell jewelry and fine weaving.

the clan they are "born to," which is the mother's clan. Second, comes the clan they are "born for"—the father's clan. If for any reason parents cannot raise their children, the mother's clan cares for the children.

Marriage within clans is forbidden, since all members of a clan are considered "sisters" or "brothers." Marriage within the clan would be regarded as incest.

There are more than seventy Diné clans. Some clans are named after elements of nature, such as Salt Clan, Reed People, and Squash People. Others are named after animals, such as Deer People and Moth People. Other clans are named after the place from which they traditionally came—Water's Edge Clan, Mountain Cove Clan. Many clans came into being as people of all sorts were adopted into the Diné nation. Paiute, Chiricahua Apache, Mojave, Tewa, Zuni, and Ute are names of indigenous people who have joined themselves to the Navajo. The Mexican clan shows the inclusive nature of the Diné. As of today, there are no clans for Anglos, Blacks, or Asians, but Navajo who have one non-Navajo parent are still "born to" or "born for" Anglo Americans, African Americans, or Asian Americans.

Members of the same clan are expected to help each other in any way needed. If people are visiting, clan members are likely to feed them and give them a place to sleep. Clans also help people to behave properly. If a member behaves shamefully, the entire group is disgraced. One of the saddest things one Diné can say about another is: "He acts as if he has no relatives."

The Navajo relate to each other through the clan structure, but they also relate in less formal ways. The Diné are particularly noted for two sports—rodeo and basketball.

Rodeos give Navajo cowgirls and cowboys an opportunity to compete, as well as get together and socialize with others in their community and with distant relatives who return for the events. As Peter Iverson relates in *The Diné*, rodeos are opportunities for "stories, anecdotes, lessons, exaggerations, and now and then what some have been rude enough to label as lies." In 1957, Navajo helped start the AIRCA—All Indian Rodeo Cowboys Association—and Diné men and women have both been outstanding contributors to the sport for decades. If parents are rodeo people, children are also likely to excel at the sport. One Navajo cowboy claims some babies are "born with boots on."

Basketball is also hugely popular in Dinétah. Navajo homes usually have a main house, a hoogan, a horse or two if they are in the country—

Elroy Harry of Shiprock, New Mexico scores a 62 on "Lover Boy" during the Diné Land Senior Rodeo Association Finals at the Northern Navajo Fair in Shiprock, New Mexico.

and a basketball hoop. In years past, Diné youngsters learned to dribble on packed dirt and not to rely on having a solid backstop. Nowadays, as Navajo Nation becomes more developed, more kids are used to playing on hardtop.

Navajo communities come out in force to cheer their local basketball teams to victory. One Navajo coach quoted in *The Diné* says: "The fans made a big difference for us. There was so much emotion that it just carried our kids like a big wave."

Between 1993 and 2001, Navajo high school teams won five out of eight state basketball championships. Diné athletes are usually not as tall as their competitors, but they outdo them in speed, skill, and attitude. Until now, only a few Diné men have played on college basketball teams. Navajo women are already known for college basketball achievement, however.

One competition in which men can't compete is the annual Miss Navajo pageant. Sasheen Hollow Horn writes about this unique event in the *Navajo Times*. The pageant began in the 1930s as an attempt by the Bureau of Indian Affairs to create interest in agricultural fairs. The early competitions were very simple—a hat was held over the heads of contestants, and whoever got the biggest cheers won. In more recent years, Miss Navajo has been seen as an ambassador for her nation. She is expected to **embody** the virtues of First Woman, Changing Woman, and White Shell Woman. As Hollow Horn writes: "Because she represents womanhood and fulfills the role of grandmother, mother, aunt and sister to the Navajo people, Miss Navajo can speak as a leader, teacher, counselor, advisor and friend."

There is no bathing suit contest for Miss Navajo; it would not encourage Diné values. The contest is open to Diné women ages eighteen to twenty-five who have never married and have no children. Contestants must be fluent in both Diné and English languages, knowledgeable in Navajo history and culture, and a high school graduate with a driver's license.

The contest lasts five days. Preliminary contests include butchering sheep, filleting mutton, and making tortillas. Then contestants must demonstrate spinning and traditional craft skills along with a modern talent. The candidates are judged for public speeches and answers to impromptu questions, both of which must be given in both Navajo and English.

The winning Miss Navajo gets a salary for the year and a tribal vehicle that she can drive for her official duties. She also gets to stay at an apartment with paid utilities in Window Rock; and she is awarded a scholarship of more than $7,500 on completion of her reign. More important than these **perks**, however, are the honor and responsibilities she receives as Miss Navajo, something people will never forget.

A Fun Way to Learn More

If you like mysteries and you want to learn more about the Navajo, you should check out Tony Hillerman's novels. Tony is a Bilagaana (Caucasian), yet he has deep understanding of Diné ways. He writes detective stories in which his heroes, Lt. Joe Leaphorn and Officer Jim Chee, pursue justice amid the mesas, deserts, and hoogans of Dinétah. Readers learn much about Diné culture—and they are kept guessing until the last page.

Navajo weaver D.Y. Begay spins wool into yarn using a traditional Navajo spindle. Most of her wool comes from her own small flock of Churro sheep. Weaving is the best known form of Navajo art.

Chapter 6

Modern Arts

"It is the handiwork of the gods."

In *The Book of the Navajo*, Raymond Locke recalls a European lady visiting America for the first time. She was at Kayenta watching a Diné woman weaving. Invited to come closer to the loom, she touched the tapestry and then spoke those words. She was not alone in her opinion. For centuries, both indigenous and non-Native people have admired Diné woven art.

"Handiwork of the gods" may be more literally true than this tourist imagined. As Locke explains:

Spider Woman instructed Navajo women how to weave on a loom which Spider Man told them how to make. Spider Woman is one of the Holy People, associated with Spider Rock in Canyon De Chelly. The crosspoles were made of sky and earth cords, the warp sticks of sun rays, the heddles of rock crystals and sheet lightning.

In the old days, Diné women always left a hole in the center of each blanket, like that in a spider's web. Traders in the early twentieth century

D. Y. Begay told Native Peoples *magazine: "It's very difficult for me to say I'm a well-known weaver or I'm a good weaver . . . I don't think I'll ever stop learning."*

refused to buy blankets with holes in them, so Diné weavers came up with a subtler custom. Today, each weaving has a "spirit outlet," a thin line from the center of the blanket to the edge. If such a spirit outlet is not included, Spider Woman will inflict the user with "blanket sickness" or mental confusion.

Apart from sacred history, it is hard to say for sure when and where the Diné began weaving. Some scholars point to weaving done by California's Indians and say the Navajo brought the skill with them from the west. Others say the Pueblo Indians taught the Diné how to weave a thousand years ago. Yet others say the Navajo were already skilled weavers when they began exchanging cultures with the Pueblos.

Before they had sheep, the Diné wove cloth from wild cotton, which grew like tall grass on the northern Arizona prairies. As soon as sheep reached the Navajo, the Diné immediately set about raising them and using their wool. As long as anyone can remember, the Diné were known as outstanding weavers, and other cultures traded for their blankets. It isn't important where they first learned the craft—what's clear is that the Navajo excel at weaving.

Weaving is a long process. First, the wool must be trimmed—sheared—off the sheep. (The favorite wool comes from Churro sheep, which the Diné have raised especially for this purpose. The fleece off a Churro sheep can be up to seven inches long.) Then the wool must be carded; two wooden blocks with comb-like teeth are pulled in opposing directions to pull the fibers into parallel lines. Next, the wool is spun into yarn. This is done with a hand spindle, like a big top rotated on the floor.

Today, most Diné weavers use natural dyes as their ancestors did. During the late 1800s and early 1900s, traders encouraged bright commercial colored dyes. These were popular at the time, but for the past fifty years, the Diné have returned to natural colors; collectors agree these are the most desirable choices. Chamizo flowers are boiled to make a deep yellow, rabbitbrush makes an earthy yellow, and prickly pear cactus makes a rose or purple dye.

The weaving itself is done on an upright loom. This is a very laborious process. A weaver will need two to three months to create an average weave four-foot by six-foot (1.2 by 1.83 meters) rug, or five to six months for an extremely fine piece. There are no shortcuts using the traditional

Diné weavers use an upright loom.

Basket of hand-spun yarn hand dyed with plants: walnut hull, onion skins (yellow and purple), cochineal, rabbitbrush, blood roots, madder roots, and black beans. D. Y. Begay does her own dyeing using natural dyes.

weaving process. Nonindigenous people, used to machine-made products, sometimes think handwoven tapestries are expensive. When one considers the time and skill involved, Diné weavers are really asking very little for their work.

The weaver is positioned in front of the loom and works with arms up-raised. Yarns stretched up and down along the length of the loom are called the warp. These are usually plain colored. Dyed yarn woven back and forth in between the warp is called the weft. Long, thin wooden rods keep the warp threads in place. A weaving comb is used to pack the wefts tightly over the warps in order to conceal them. Each weaver keeps the entire design for a tapestry in her head.

There are approximately sixteen different styles of Diné weaving. Some of the best known are:

• The Teec Nos Pos and Red Mesa style weaving, which is almost Asian looking, with intricate many-colored designs.

- The Two Grey Hills and Ganado Red tapestries, which are geometric in design and made with subdued colors of undyed wool.
- The Tree of Life, the most common design, which portrays birds perched on cornstalks and trees growing out of baskets.
- Yei designs, which are pictures of supernatural beings from Diné sacred tradition.

Until recently, Diné weavers did not sign their work. Navajo woven art has been known by the place where it is made more than by the maker. In the twenty-first century, however, Navajo weavers are making rugs even more complex, more beautiful, and more creative than did their mothers and grandmothers. They are also gaining recognition by name for their art.

Marilou Schultz was born into a family of weavers extending back three generations. She has an advanced degree in mathematics, and some of her rugs are a combination of traditional materials and designs inspired by computer chips. Florence Riggs comes from a distinguished weaving fam-

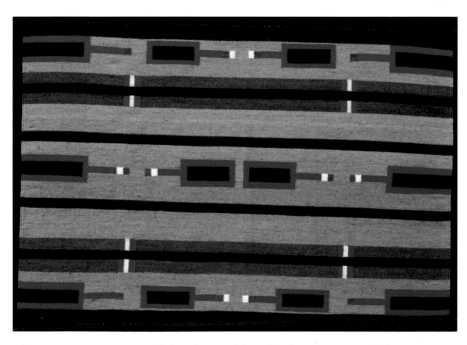

This D. Y. Begay rug is titled Dakota Style. *The design is inspired from a Cheyenne motif. The artist enjoys incorporating simple and bold designs into her weavings.*

Stores in Gallup, New Mexico, are the most important outlets for Navajo art. Gallup is located near the Navajo Nation and Zuni Pueblo. The city has more than a hundred trading posts, galleries, and shops that sell American Indian art.

ily; her grandmother, Laura Nez, was famous for her woven art. Florence recently wove a tapestry picturing twenty-one different dinosaurs. After the tragedy of September 11, 2001, Arlene Yazzie wove a huge American flag tapestry, eight feet (2.44 meters) long and five feet (1.5 meters) high.

D. Y. Begay is a Navajo weaver who takes her inspirations from the beautiful landscape around her hoogan. She raises a small herd of Churro sheep for her wool. In May of 2000, she and another Diné woman traveled to an indigenous community in Guatemala. Guatemala's Indians, like the Navajo, are famous for woven art. She exchanged techniques with women of the Q'uechi tribe she met there. Later that year, she was also able to visit with indigenous people in Peru. She purchased natural dyes to compare with her own. On another trip, she and other Diné weavers went to Corsica to exchange knowledge of sheepherding and weaving techniques. The Diné have been exchanging artistic techniques with other cultures for centuries, and now, in the twenty-first century, that exchange has become global.

The Diné are also famous for their silver artwork. Despite their warfare with the Spanish, the Navajo learned to appreciate Spanish silver work in the eighteenth century. The famous squash blossom necklace and conch belt designs were inspired by Spanish and Mexican artists. Contact with Anglo Americans in the late nineteenth century refined the Navajo's jewelry making skills.

The first Navajo silversmith known by name was Atsidi Sani. In 1872, another smith, Atsidi Chon, moved to Zuni and taught Lanyade, who was the first Zuni silver worker. Lanyade then taught Sikyatala, who was the first Hopi to work in silver. Today, the Navajo, Zuni, and Hopi are all known for their silver crafts.

The classic style Navajo jewelry was made from melted American silver coins. This became illegal in 1890. After that, Diné jewelers used Mexican pesos, which were also made of fine silver. In 1930, however, Mexico made it illegal to export coins, and since then Navajo jewelers have purchased sterling silver from silver refineries. Turquoise and other precious stones are also used in Navajo jewelry designs.

Diné artists have also gained a reputation for painting on canvas and paper. In 1932, the Bureau of Indian Affairs established an art class at the Santa Fe Indian School. Before that, few Navajo artists had been able to afford paint supplies. The Santa Fe School at first taught sketching and watercolor painting on paper. Soon, Navajo painters proved their skills with the whole range of painting techniques. Andy Tsinjannie, R. C. Gorman,

An "old style" Navajo jeweler's workshop includes a variety of stamps.

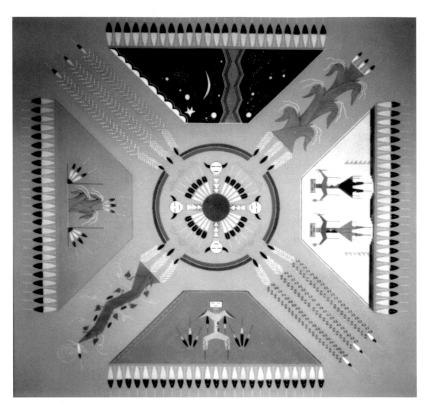

Sandpaintings made for artistic expressions are different in design from those used in sacred ceremonies. Layers of glue are carefully applied to form a permanent design.

Harrison Begay, Charlie Lee, and David Johns are all noted Navajo painters.

Dennis Arviso is a Navajo artist with an unusual style of painting. In 1986, he was in a serious accident that left him a *quadriplegic*. Refusing to be discouraged, Arviso pursued an artistic career. He paints landscapes by holding the paintbrush in his mouth. It may take weeks for him to complete a picture, but today Dennis Arviso is an established artist. He often visits Navajo schools to demonstrate his painting technique to children.

Navajo sandpainting is a form of sacred expression that has developed into a commercial art form. Sacred sandpaintings (properly referred to as dry paintings, as discussed in chapter four) are created and destroyed in hoogans during healing ceremonies. They are never kept permanently.

Sandpaintings for artistic expression and sales are different designs from those used in sacred ceremonies. They are created on a piece of particleboard or plywood. Finely crushed stones—some natural, some permanently dyed—are applied to glue on the base. More glue is painted on top of that layer, and then more sand is deposited. The layer of glue must be applied just right; if it's too thick or too thin, the final product will not be durable. It is tricky getting the sand particles in the right place on the glue. Most sandpainters place a small amount of sand in the palm of their hand below the second finger. Guided by the thumb, the sand trickles off the index finger onto the picture. The sand must fall at an even speed or the picture will be ruined. Some sandpainters sketch designs by pencil before creating the final artwork; others work only by eye. Like weavers and silversmiths, sandpainting artists are creating finer and finer works.

One of Betty Manygoats' pots.

A Navajo weaver takes strands of wool and blends them into something of great beauty and magic; warp and weft combine into a pattern, and the pattern tells a story and has a spirit. This pattern then becomes a piece of the culture and has a life of its own.

From *The Scalpel and the Silver Bear* by Lori Arviso Alvord and Elizabeth Cohen Van Pelt.

Art collectors do not regard Diné pottery as highly as that of the Pueblos. Traditional Navajo pots were not painted and were made to be functional rather than artistic. Recently, Diné craftsmen *have* begun making "horse-hair" style pottery and pottery made from molds with fine designs etched (scratched) onto them. Although neither of these are traditional Diné art forms, they can be well made and aesthetically pleasing.

Betty Manygoats stands out as a Diné potter who has achieved award-winning results making pottery using traditional Diné techniques. She was taught to make pottery by her grandmother. Her pots are covered with pine or pinion pitch before a final heating. This is a traditional Diné technique that makes pots watertight and gives them a pleasing shiny finish. The clay fires to a caramel brown.

Manygoats lives in a remote part of the Navajo Nation. She began making pottery as a way to provide for her nine daughters and one son. Twenty years ago she was inspired to add horned toad designs to her work. Many Diné consider the horned toad bad luck, but Betty Manygoats is Christian and does not share those fears. She doesn't speak English, but that hasn't stopped her from being profiled in books, winning awards at art shows, and teaching art to students at Tuba High School. Her favorite art students are her children, several of whom have also become highly regarded potters.

On the Navajo Nation, where jobs are in short supply, one out of every three Navajo work full- or part-time as an artist. Unfortunately, there are many fakes who sell jewelry, weaving, and other art forms that copy Diné styles. According to some estimates, half the sales that should go to Native artists actually pay for frauds. Buyers are cheated; they are getting something far less valuable than what they paid for. Even worse, American Indian artists are being cheated out of their livelihood.

When you buy Native American art, make sure it is genuine. The best way to do this is to buy from the artist himself or herself. Meeting Navajo artists and conversing with them is fun. If you can't do that, buy from traders and art dealers who have represented Indian artists for many

Award-winning Navajo weaver Lorraine Black of Mexican Hat, Utah, made this splendid basket to commemorate the opening of the 2002 Olympics. It is now in the collection of the Southwest Indian Foundation in Gallup, New Mexico.

years. They should be able to tell you details about who made a piece of art. If you buy genuine Navajo art, you are helping the artist and his or her family earn a living—and you bring part of the beauty of Diné life into your own home.

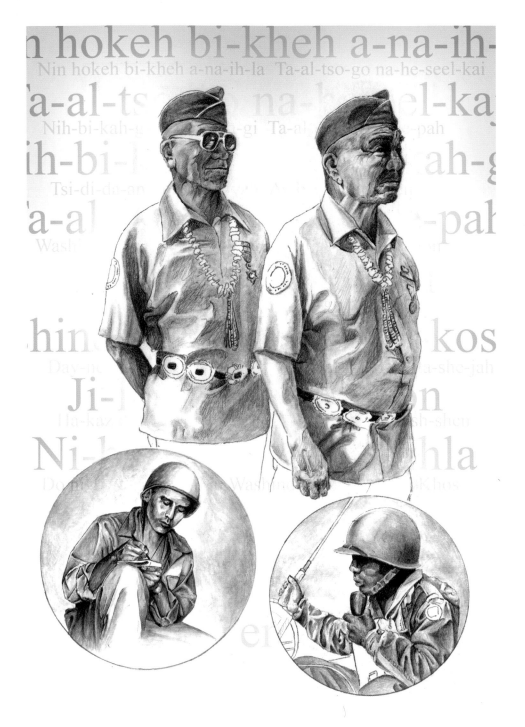

Navajo Code Talkers made tremendous contributions to American victory in the Pacific Theater during World War II.

Chapter 7

Contributions to the World

They were America's best-kept secret during World War II—so secret that their special mission remained hidden with the government until 1968. They gave everything a citizen could sacrifice for his country, and most of them died without recognition. They are known as the Navajo Code Talkers.

During World War II, 3,600 Diné men and twelve women served in the armed forces. They all served nobly—but a special group had a unique mission.

Both sides in the war used codes to coordinate attacks on enemy targets and communicate troop movements. When Japan attacked Pearl Harbor, they had apparently broken American codes. Knowing what the enemy was about to do made the critical difference in many battles. Navajo Marines created a code in their own language, which was known by very few non-Navajo. The Navajo Code Talkers chose one word in Navajo to

Patriotic support for America is strong on the Navajo Nation.

represent each letter of the alphabet. Navajo words were also used to represent military terms. An observation plane was an "owl." A "buzzard" (bomber) dropped "eggs" (bombs). A tank destroyer was a "tortoise killer." Military units were named after Diné clans. The code was so vital that Code Talkers were expected to die rather than face capture and torture by the enemy.

The Code Talkers were invaluable to U.S. operations in the **Pacific Theater**. Major Howard M. Connor, communications officer for the Fifth Marine Division, commented: "Without the Navajos, the Marines would never have taken Iwo Jima." Iwo Jima was the biggest, bloodiest battle of World War II, the decisive battle in America's strategy of "island hopping" troops toward the Japanese islands. There is a famous statue of Marines raising the American flag atop Iwo Jima Island. One of the men commemorated by that statue is Ira Robinson Hayes, a Pima Indian.

Navajo Code Talker Teddy Draper Sr. talked to the *Navajo Times* about Iwo Jima. Draper, who was seventy-eight in 2002, vividly remembers February 19, 1945. "It was almost a suicide mission," he says. "I saw red, bloody sand. There was all kinds of noises—machine guns, grenades, land mines, airplane bombs." As the Marines crawled up on the beach, they

Next to the Navajo Nation government complex and in front of the majestic
Window Rock Formation is the Navajo Nation Veterans' Memorial Park.

realized necessary equipment for the Code Talkers' radios had been left behind. Draper was selected to go back and get them. "There were millions of bullets that were on my back and head," he recalls. Thousands of men died in the battle, including six Navajo. Corporal Teddy Draper was promoted to Sergeant Major. He couldn't tell what he had done during the war, since it was kept secret by the government. He was wounded in the war, losing 50 percent of his sight and hearing, and was unable to find work afterward. He still is affected by his experiences:

> At this time of year [the date of the battle of Iwo Jima] I get really sick with headaches as I hear the noise, the boys chattering and the explosions. I think about it and I think about all my friends who went to the battle of Iwo Jima. Sometimes I can't see, I can't hear; all that I hear is that noise in my head.

In 2001, after years of secrecy, the Code Talkers were finally acknowledged for their heroism. On July 26, 2001, President George W. Bush awarded the Congressional Gold Medal to the original Navajo Code Talkers for their outstanding contribution to the World War II effort. The Congressional Gold Medal is one of the highest awards the U.S. government can bestow on her citizens. President Bush said the Code Talkers had saved thousands of lives and helped win the war. Only five of the original twenty-nine Code Talkers are still alive, but Allen June, Lloyd Oliver, Chester Nez, and John Brown Jr. were able to attend the ceremony. Later in the year, silver medals were awarded to the four hundred Code Talkers who followed the original twenty-nine.

Shortly after the bestowing of these awards, MGM studios released the movie *Windtalkers*. In the film, Adam Beach stars as Navajo Code Talker Ben Yahzee, and Nicholas Cage plays a Marine officer. Adam Beach is a member of the Saulteaux Tribe from Dog Creek Reserve in Canada. He had trouble trying to speak the Diné language throughout the movie. Beach said Navajo is the most difficult—and most beautiful language—with which he has ever worked.

Patriotism is evident throughout Dinétah. Next to the Navajo Nation government complex and in front of stunningly beautiful Window Rock formation is the Navajo Nation Veterans' Memorial Park. The park commemorates "those men and women who gave the ultimate sacrifice in the service of our country, our land and the Diné way of life; those who bravely fought and have since deceased; those who stood ready in times of peace and those who are still holding vigilance for peace and democracy."

A young woman at the cash register in the Subway restaurant notices a young man in uniform and starts a conversation. Her family has two generations serving in three branches of the armed services. She's proud of the contributions they have made to America. Her feelings could be echoed elsewhere throughout Dinétah.

The contributions of the Diné people to the world are by no means limited to the armed services. Lori Alvord is associate dean for student affairs and minority affairs as well as assistant professor of surgery at Dartmouth Medical School in New Hampshire. She is the first Navajo woman surgeon. Debora Lynn Norris, who is Navajo and Blackfeet, is the youngest member of the Arizona State Legislature and one of the first two Native American women to serve in the Arizona House of Representatives. Sandra Begay-Campbell is a member of the Navajo Nation and former executive director of the American Indian Science and Engineering Society.

R. C. Gorman is considered by many to be the most important American Indian artist today. Rudolph Carl Gorman was born in Chinle, Arizona. Raised by his grandmother, Gorman lived in a hoogan during his childhood and had little experience with the world outside of the Navajo Nation. His grandmother ignited Gorman's imagination by telling him Diné oral tradi-

The Diné College campus is situated in Tsaile, Arizona, near the scenic Lukachukai and Chuska Mountains. Diné College is the first tribally controlled community college in the country. The campus features a six-story, hoogan-shaped cultural center.

tions and acquainting him with his artistic ancestors. In 1958, he received the first scholarship given by the Navajo Nation for study outside the United States. He took classes at Mexico City College, where he was exposed to artists who helped him form his distinctive art.

Gorman's paintings are noted for a bold free-flowing style and vivid colors. The *New York Times* describes him as "the Picasso of American Indian artists." Most of his drawings are of women. As a child in Chinle, he drew a "naked lady" and was promptly spanked by both his teacher and his mother. If only they could have foreseen his success! R. C. Gorman has won many awards. He keeps them in a closet in his home, "because" he jokes, "the white natives might steal them."

Outstanding Navajo individuals are not the only ones to make contributions to our world; Navajo organizations have also done their part. Diné College, for instance, is a landmark in Native American education. When it opened in 1968, it was the first college established by American Indians in the United States. Nestled amid the scenic Lukachukai and Chuska Moun-

The New York Times *describes Navajo painter R. C. Gorman as "the Picasso of American Indian Artists."*

The Navajo people are good stewards of their land.

tains in Tsaile, Arizona, the campus features a six-story cultural center shaped like a hoogan with mirrored glass panels. A well-equipped modern campus spreads out beside the cultural center. Degrees in computer science, business, psychology, environmental sciences, and many other subjects are offered at the college. Along with more common subjects, Diné College has courses in Navajo language, culture, and history. Tribal colleges like Diné College have proven to be vastly more successful with indigenous students than other schools. Colleges started and run by Indians are making a real impact in the educational achievement of Native Americans, and Diné College was a model for their success.

Far away from Dinétah, the National Museum of the American Indian (with buildings in New York City and Washington, D.C.) holds great promise for indigenous people around the country. The mission of the museum is to work directly with Native communities throughout the hemisphere, learning their stories and traditions and developing the museum along with them. Even the design of the building was done with American Indian input. The museum, affiliated with the Smithsonian Institution, will include

Leonda Levchuck is proud to work for the new National Museum of the American Indian.

artifacts from Alaska in the north to Tierra del Fuego, which is the southern tip of South America.

Leonda Levchuck is a Navajo young woman who was born in Gallup, New Mexico. After graduating from Pennsylvania State University in 1997, she was hired to work as a public affairs assistant with the National Museum of the American Indian. She has loved her job from the start. In September of 2002, she participated in the powwow on the National Mall, and she was excited about this event for two reasons: It let the people of the United States see that Native cultures are alive and well. And it also let Washington, D.C., know the National Museum of the American Indian is being built. The museum covers the last available spot on the National Mall and should be completed in the fall of 2004.

Dr. Lori Arviso Alvord is another Navajo woman who is doing much, both for her own people and for the world. Dr. Alvord grew up on the reservation in New Mexico but left to attend Stanford University Medical School. Fewer women than men become surgeons, and even fewer Native Americans achieve this goal—but Dr. Alvord broke through the barriers to become the first Navajo woman surgeon. Today she works in Gallop, New

> I realized that although I was a good surgeon, I was not always a good healer. I went back to the healers of my tribe to learn what a surgical residency could not teach me. From them I heard a resounding message: Everything in life is connected. Learn to understand the bonds between humans, spirit, and nature. Realize that our illness and our healing alike come from maintaining strong and healthy relationships in every aspect of our lives.
>
> From *The Scalpel and the Silver Bear* by Lori Arviso Alvord and Elizabeth Cohen Van Pelt.

Mexico, bringing modern medicine to her people, even as she works to integrate Diné healing beliefs with her medical practice. In her autobiography, *The Scalpel and the Silver Bear,* she writes:

> If modern medicine is lost—and many believe it is—perhaps it can find its way by looking to the traditions and beliefs of some of America's first inhabitants. It is my hope and vision that groups of people can learn from one another—that the culture of medicine can learn from the culture of Native Americans, and that both can be richer from the experience.

Diné like Dr. Alvord, Leonda Levchuck, R. C. Gorman, and the Code Talkers have all done their part to fight for freedom, to work for education, and to enrich our culture with knowledge and wisdom from the past. North America would not be the same without the Navajo—and neither would our entire world.

The Navajo Nation has preserved pieces of the past for us all to enjoy.

Chapter 8

Challenges for Today, Hopes for the Future

Teri Silversmith is passionate about her work, because what she does makes a real difference. Her job is to process requests for new homes or safe heating for homes. The applicants are Navajo tribal members; most of them are elderly.

She has a stack of "before" and "after" files. One photo, for example, shows an elderly woman living in a partially burned hoogan with holes in the roof. The follow-up file is quite different: the same woman is in a neatly made frame home of modern construction. Another picture shows a disabled man in a small house with a woodstove pieced together from an old oil drum and pipes, obviously one step away from disaster. The "after" picture shows the same man in the same house, but now with a neat, fuel-efficient stove safely installed. Teri talks about each case with affection and obvious pride; she is glad for the ways her organization has helped her people.

Teri Silversmith works for the Southwest Indian Foundation in Gallup, New Mexico. She helps Navajo tribal members attain new homes and safe heating.

Teri works for the Southwest Indian Foundation in Gallup, New Mexico. The Foundation assists American Indians, with priority given to the elderly, handicapped, and families with dependent children. It works mostly with the Navajo, but it assists Pueblo tribes in the area as well. Although the Southwest Foundation is a Catholic organization founded by a Franciscan priest, it is "not a *propagating* arm of the Catholic Church." It serves Indian families in need regardless of their religion.

There is, unfortunately, plenty of need in Navajo country. The biggest problem continues to be poverty. In 2003, 46 percent of Navajo were unemployed. Many people on the Navajo Nation live in remote rural areas and most of these still have no electricity, 54 percent lack complete plumbing facilities, and 48 percent have no telephone. Many reservation roads are unpaved, and they may be impassible during the wintertime.

Diabetes is a debilitating disease for many Native Americans, one that often results in kidney failure and blindness. Navajo suffer from this illness twelve times more than the rest of the American population.

More than half the Diné live in what is termed "distressed housing." That may mean they lack means of waste disposal or running water, or they are missing windows or have leaking roofs. Inadequate heating and lack of insulation are serious issues in Dinétah, where the high elevation brings extreme cold on winter nights. Most Navajo burn wood to heat their homes. Some cannot afford real woodstoves and instead use sawed-off water heaters and other crude contraptions. Hoogans, constructed on wood frames, can catch fire and burn down in only minutes.

The Southwest Foundation office where Teri Silversmith works has several programs that help with these needs. One program accepts contributions from the public and uses these charitable funds to buy new woodstoves for homes needing them. (The cost of a new woodstove is $355.) The Foundation also helps with housing assistance for Navajo diabetes patients who need to relocate in order to receive *dialysis* treatment.

In 1998, the Southwest Foundation teamed up with the Air Force Academy in Colorado Springs in Operation Good Neighbor, a program to build houses. The Navajo Housing Authority donates materials, the Southwest Foundation does all the paperwork, and Air Force cadets provide the labor. Cadets have built at least three houses on the Navajo Nation each year. In 2002, they built seven and plan for fifteen in 2003. The homes they build—using modern materials—are eight-sided hoogans. Another Foundation building project employs recovering alcoholics, who have trouble finding work, to build new housing for needy people. The Southwest Foundation seeks to give "a hand up rather than a handout" to people.

The Navajo people are seeking to create more jobs in Dinétah. Crownpoint Institute of Technology (CIT) in Crownpoint, New Mexico, had a creative idea and started an elk herd. Elk are the best investment today in livestock, worth ten times as much as cattle. Elk antlers can be sold and ground up for popular herbal medicine, and since antlers grow back year

Rhonda Ray, of the Southwest Indian Foundation, poses with "Chase." Twenty-eight outstanding Indian artists have worked on this painted pony in order to raise money that will pay for $25,000 in scholarships for emerging young Indian artists. Rhonda affectionately calls the pony "Chase," since he will help young people to pursue their dreams.

Destruction of culture and resulting loss of pride, combined with poverty, has caused an unfortunate number of American Indians to have substance abuse problems. Drinking alcohol is not permitted on Navajo lands, but many Diné go to Gallup, New Mexico to buy alcohol.

after year, they are a profitable, renewable resource. Crownpoint's elk industry also provides jobs.

Tourism to the Navajo Nation has been popular for decades, but in the past, non-Navajo living in and near the nation have made most of the money. The Diné are now working to develop new tourism businesses owned by members of the Nation. Navajo guides provide exceptional knowledge to tours of Canyon De Chelly and Monument Valley. Will Tsosie's Coyote Pass Hospitality advertises "off the beaten track escapades are our specialty." Guests can stay overnight in an old-style hoogan, heated by a woodstove. Tsosie guarantees that "outhouses are provided!" Coyote Pass Hospitality may be just the thing if your family is tired of staying in motels that all look the same.

May it be beautiful before me.
May it be beautiful behind me.
May it be beautiful below me.
May it be beautiful above me.
May it be beautiful all around me.

In beauty it is finished.

—Navajo Night Chant

A century ago, photographer Edward Curtis introduced his book of Navajo portraits with a picture he titled *Vanishing Race*. After the American government's attempts to do away with the Diné in the nineteenth century, his title may have seemed likely to come true. Despite all their hardship, however, at the start of the twenty-first century, the Navajo should more aptly be called "the Flourishing Race." The majority of the Diné people are younger than twenty-five years old. The Navajo struggle with lack of jobs and resulting poverty, but many other groups in America face similar problems. At the same time, they have strong cultural traditions, clan connections, and a sense of their unique identity. They know how to confront and overcome challenges.

On a fall afternoon, a friend and I stop in at Cool Runnings, in St. Michael's Arizona, just West of Window Rock on the Navajo Nation. In some respects, it is like other modern music stores. There are tons of CDs and the staff is good at finding discs that shoppers can't locate. Bright T-shirts hang on racks; one shirt looks like an Old Navy design but instead says "Old Navajo." Other items are also different from most music stores; for example, the store sells silver, turquoise, and other materials for making jewelry. Examples of traditional Diné artwork—sandpaintings, jewelry, and weaving—are for sale. There are packets of sage, dried leaves that are burned as incense for purification in ceremonies.

This store is uniquely Navajo, like no music store I've been to anywhere else. It says a lot about Navajo life. The Diné—especially younger members—are not afraid of progress. They are striving to grasp the future by the horns and make the most of it. That does not, however, mean they are blending into non-Navajo cultures or losing their sense of Diné identity. Like the rest of us in the twenty-first century, the Navajo have many challenges to face and overcome. Without a doubt, these challenges will change them. They will not be the same a century from now—but they will still be distinctively Navajo. As we move forward into the future, the Diné will continue to walk in beauty.

> People have power to upset the Circle of Life. We have made weapons that kill more game than we need. We have farmed land that should have been left wild. We have dug ditches and built dams. All these things have changed the life around us, and in the end have changed us too.
>
> —George Blueeyes, Navajo medicine man

Dance advertisements near Window Rock demonstrate the vitality of Navajo youth.

Edward Curtis's Vanishing Race.

As the Navajo Nation enters the twenty-first century, they have maintained their deep roots in their land and history.

Further Reading

Alvord, Lori Arviso and Elizabeth Cohen Van Pelt. *The Scalpel and the Silver Bear*. New York: Bantam, 2000.

Iverson, Peter. *Diné: A History of the Navajos*. Albuquerque: University of New Mexico Press, 2002.

Locke, Raymond Friday. *The Book of the Navajo*. Los Angeles: Mankind Publishing Company, 2001.

McIntosh, Kenneth. *Apache*. Philadelphia, Penn.: Mason Crest, 2004.

O'Bryan, Aileen. *Navajo Indian Myths*. New York: Dover, 1994.

Trimble, Stephen. *The People: Indians of the American Southwest*. Santa Fe, N.M.: School of American Research, 2000.

Weatherford, Jack. *Indian Givers: How the Indians of the Americas Transformed the World*. New York: Fawcett Columbine, 1990.

For More Information

DY Begay the Navajo Weaver
www.amug.org/ ~ dybegay/

Miss Navajo Nation
www.missnavajo.org

The Navajo Central.org Web site
ourworld.compuserve.com/homepages/larry_dilucchio/homepage.htm

Official Web site of the Navajo Nation
www.navajo.org

Publisher's Note:

The Web sites listed on this page were active at the time of publication. The publisher is not responsible for Web sites that have changed their address or discontinued operation since the date of publication. The publisher will review and update the Web sites upon each reprint.

Glossary

adjudication: The process of settling a matter using a judge.

adobe: A brick or building material made of sun-dried earth and straw.

anthropologist: Someone who studies human beings in relation to their distribution, origin, and the relationship of races, environmental and social relationships, and culture.

apprentices: People who are learning a trade or skill by working with an experienced person for a specified time period.

archaeologists: Scientists who study physical remains to understand the lives of people in the distant past.

artifacts: Objects created by humans usually for practical purposes.

atrocities: Acts that are extremely cruel, wicked, or brutal.

Bureau of Indian Affairs: The government agency that acts as an advocate for Indian needs.

bureaucrats: Members of an administrative policy-making group.

criteria: The standards by which judgments or decisions are based.

detoxification: The process of removing addictive and poisonous substances from the body.

diabetes: A disease caused by inadequate production or use of insulin.

dialysis: The process of cleaning the blood when a person's kidneys are not working sufficiently.

diverse: The characteristic of being different from one another.

divination: The art that attempts to foretell future events or discover hidden information usually through the interpretation of omens or by supernatural powers.

embody: To represent an idea or power in human form.

extermination: The process of getting rid of something completely, usually by killing.

fertility: The ability to grow new life.

Franciscan friar: A member of the Order of Friars Minor, a Catholic group founded by St. Francis of Assisi.

germination: The process of getting something to sprout or develop.

Great Depression: A period of low economic activity and increasing levels of unemployment that occurred from October 1929 until about 1939.

hoogans: The original and unique Navajo homes, made of logs and dirt, having six or eight sides. Nowadays the hoogan is still the center of ceremonial life, and important public buildings are shaped like hoogans. Most non-Navajos spell this "hogan."

indigenous: Something that is found naturally in an area.

infrastructure: The system of public works, including roads and utilities, of a country, state, or region.

medicine men: Priestly healers.

mesas: Isolated, relatively flat elevations that resemble tables (mesas is Spanish for tables).

neutering: Making a male animal unable to impregnate a female animal.

nomadic: Moving from place to place.

Pacific Theater: Battle sites of World War II that were in or near the Pacific Ocean.

pacifists: People who are strongly opposed to war or violence as a way of solving conflicts.

perks: Perquisites. Privileges or profits that are in addition to wages or salary.

perseverance: The act of persisting despite discouragement; stick-to-itiveness.

progressive: Relating to moving forward, advancing, improving.

propagating: Causing to spread out and to affect a larger area.

prospectors: People who went looking for gold or other valuable minerals.

quadriplegic: Someone who has the inability to use his or her arms and legs.

radioactive: Having to do with elements or isotopes that exhibit the spontaneous emission of energetic particles by the disintegration of their nuclei.

revered: Held in high esteem.

sacramental: Using a concrete, tangible object to reveal some aspect of the spiritual world.

spaying: Performing surgery to make a female animal unable to have offspring.

sweat house: A building used for ritual purposes that is heated by steam produced by pouring water over hot rocks.

traditional: Having to do with the culture and beliefs of one's ancestors.

uranium: A heavy, radioactive element.

Index

Alvard, Lori 80, 83, 91
Anasazis 17
Ashley, Ray 36, 45
Athapascan 19, 29
Aviso, Dennis 70

Barboncito 22, 24
basketball 59–60
Begay, D.Y. 62, 64, 66, 67, 68
Begay-Campbell, Sandra 80
Bureau of Indian Affairs 27, 28,
    60–61, 69

Canyon de Chelly 15, 18, 29, 63
Canyon del Muerto 18
Carson, Kit 18, 22–23, 33
Christianity 11, 26, 46, 47, 50, 52, 53,
    86
clans 16, 17, 58–59, 76, 89
coal 31, 32–33
Code Talkers 30, 74–76, 78–79, 83
Collier, John 27–29
creation story 12–17
Curtis, Edward 15, 20, 42, 88, 90

diabetes 86, 87
Diné Alliance 33
Diné College 31, 56, 79, 81–82
Draper, Teddy Sr. 76, 78

Eagle Plume 44
education 31, 35, 56, 79, 81–82
elk industry 87–88

four sacred materials 14–15, 17
four sacred mountains 14–15, 17, 57,
    58
fraudulent Indian artwork 72

Gorman, R.C. 78, 80, 81, 83

Holy People 14, 15, 44, 46, 47, 63
hoogans 11, 12, 14, 15, 44, 46, 47,
    48, 55–58, 59, 61, 68, 70, 79, 80,
    81, 86, 87, 94

hüzhü 17, 39, 44
Hubbell, Don Lorenzo 25

Indian Agency schools 26–27

jewelry making 69, 89
Joe, Oreland 30
Jim, Harrison 44

language 19–20, 27–28, 35, 36,
    37–38, 53, 82
Levchuk, Leonda 82–83
Locke, Raymond Friday 45

MacDonald, Peter 32
Manygoats, Betty 71, 72
medicine men 35, 42, 47, 49, 50, 89,
    94
military service 29, 30, 74–76,
    78–80
Miss Navajo pageant 54, 60–61

Narbono, Antonio 18
National Museum of the American
    Indian 82–83
Native American Church 47, 50,
    51–52, 53
Navajo Business Council 27, 37–38
Navajo Nation Code 37
Navajo Nation Veterans' Memorial
    Park 77, 79
Navajo Veterinary Program 39–40
Nez, Laura 68
Norris, Debora Lynn 80

oil 27, 37
Operation Good Neighbor 87
oral traditions 12–17, 80

painters 69–70
patriotism 11, 29, 76
peacemaking 39
peyote 47, 52
pottery 72
poverty 11, 26, 86, 88, 89

Ray, Rhonda 87
Riggs, Florence 67, 68
rodeo 21, 59, 60

Salabye, Tova 40
sand painting 44, 45, 47, 49, 50–51,
    70–71, 89
Schultz, Marilou 67
sheep 20, 21, 25, 28–29, 33, 62, 64, 68
Shirley, Joe 35–36
Silversmith, Teri 85–86, 87
silver work 21, 68–69, 71
Sings 49
slavery 21
sovereignty 37
Spanish 18, 21, 24, 52, 69
Spider Woman 13, 14, 15, 63, 64
spiritual beliefs 43–53
spiritual leaders 44
sports 59
substance abuse 36, 39, 43–44, 88
sweat lodges 44, 47, 57

trade 17, 25–26, 63–64, 68
tribal council 36, 37
tribal government 35–41
Tsosie, Shaunda Mae 54
Tsosie, Will 88

unemployment 35, 86, 89
uranium 30
U.S. government 20, 24, 26, 29, 30,
    36, 37, 79

voting rights 29–30

warfare 20, 21, 68
Ways 49–50, 51
weaving 13, 14, 15, 21, 25, 58, 62,
    63–68, 71, 72, 73, 89
Window Rock 10, 34, 38, 58, 61, 77, 89
witchcraft 50, 52
women, in politics 37

Yazzie, Arlene 68

Biographies

Kenneth McIntosh is a pastor and his wife, Marsha, is a schoolteacher. They both took leave from their regular jobs to work on this series. Formerly, Kenneth worked as a junior high teacher in Los Angeles, California. He wrote Clergy for the Mason Crest series "Careers with Character." The McIntoshes live in upstate New York and have two children, Jonathan and Eirené. They are grateful for the opportunity this work has given them to travel and meet with many wonderful Native people.

Martha McCollough received her bachelor's and master's degrees in anthropology at the University of Alaska-Fairbanks, and she now teaches at the University of Nebraska. Her areas of study are contemporary Native American issues, ethnohistory, and the political and economic issues that surround encounters between North American Indians and Euroamericans.

Benjamin Stewart, a graduate of Alfred University, is a freelance photographer and graphic artist. He traveled across North America to take the photographs included in this series.

DATE